YORK NOTES

When We Are Married

J.B. Priestley

Note by Paul Nye

Longman York Press

Paul Nye is hereby identified as author of this work in accordance with Section 77 of the Copyright, Designs and Patents Act 1988

YORK PRESS
322 Old Brompton Road, London SW5 9JH

PEARSON EDUCATION LIMITED
Edinburgh Gate, Harlow,
Essex CM20 2JE, United Kingdom
Associated companies, branches and representatives throughout the world

First published 2000

ISBN 0-582-43180-8

Designed by Vicki Pacey
Phototypeset by Gem Graphics, Trenance, Mawgan Porth, Cornwall
Colour reproduction and film output by Spectrum Colour
Produced by Addison Wesley Longman China Limited, Hong Kong

C ONTENTS

Preface   **4**

PART ONE

I NTRODUCTION   How to Study a Play   **5**
   J.B. Priestley's Background   **6**
   Context & Setting   **10**

PART TWO

S UMMARIES   General Summary   **14**
   Detailed Summaries, Comment,
     Glossaries & Tests   **17**
     Act I   **17**
     Act II   **28**
     Act III   **36**

PART THREE

C OMMENTARY   Themes   **44**
   Structure   **47**
   Characters   **49**
   Language & Style   **56**

PART FOUR

S TUDY SKILLS   How to Use Quotations   **58**
   Essay Writing   **59**
   Sample Essay Plan & Questions   **62**

PART FIVE

C ULTURAL CONNECTIONS
   Broader Perspectives   **65**
Literary Terms   **67**
Test Answers   **68**

PREFACE

York Notes are designed to give you a broader perspective on works of literature studied at GCSE and equivalent levels. We have carried out extensive research into the needs of the modern literature student prior to publishing this new edition. Our research showed that no existing series fully met students' requirements. Rather than present a single authoritative approach, we have provided alternative viewpoints, empowering students to reach their own interpretations of the text. York Notes provide a close examination of the work and include biographical and historical background, summaries, glossaries, analyses of characters, themes, structure and language, cultural connections and literary terms.

If you look at the Contents page you will see the structure for the series. However, there's no need to read from the beginning to the end as you would with a novel, play, poem or short story. Use the Notes in the way that suits you. Our aim is to help you with your understanding of the work, not to dictate how you should learn.

York Notes are written by English teachers and examiners, with an expert knowledge of the subject. They show you how to succeed in coursework and examination assignments, guiding you through the text and offering practical advice. Questions and comments will extend, test and reinforce your knowledge. Attractive colour design and illustrations improve clarity and understanding, making these Notes easy to use and handy for quick reference.

York Notes are ideal for:
- Essay writing
- Exam preparation
- Class discussion

The author of this Note is Paul Nye. He is an English graduate of Oxford University and has taught English Language and Literature to GCSE and 'A' level in Independent and State schools. He has also been a Moderator and Examiner for a major examining board.

The text used in these Notes is the Heineman Educational edition in the Hereford Play series, with an introduction by E.R. Wood (1971).

Health Warning: **This study guide will enhance your understanding, but should not replace the reading of the original text and/or study in class.**

PART ONE

INTRODUCTION

HOW TO STUDY A PLAY

You have bought this book because you wanted to study a play on your own. This may supplement classwork.

- Drama is a special 'kind' of writing (the technical term is 'genre') because it needs a performance in the theatre to arrive at a full interpretation of its meaning. When reading a play you have to imagine how it should be performed; the words alone will not be sufficient. Think of gestures and movements.

- Drama is always about conflict of some sort (it may be below the surface). Identify the conflicts in the play and you will be close to identifying the large ideas or themes which bind all the parts together.

- Make careful notes on themes, characters, plot and any sub-plots of the play.

- Playwrights find non-realistic ways of allowing an audience to see into the minds and motives of their characters. The 'soliloquy', in which a character speaks directly to the audience, is one such device. Does the play you are studying have any such passages?

- Which characters do you like or dislike in the play? Why? Do your sympathies change as you see more of these characters?

- Think of the playwright writing the play. Why were these particular arrangements of events, these particular sets of characters and these particular speeches chosen?

Studying on your own requires self-discipline and a carefully thought-out work plan in order to be effective. Good luck.

Historical perspective

J.B. Priestley – John Boynton Priestley, known simply as Jack to his family and friends, was born in Bradford, Yorkshire on 13 September 1894 and died on 14 August 1984. Bradford – the Bruddersford of *The Good Companions* and *When We Are Married*, was entirely the product of the Industrial Revolution. In less than a hundred years its population had grown over fivefold. This gave rise to the background problems and politics that influenced the Priestley family. His father was a schoolmaster and had been to college. This was a great achievement in those times when the usual course for an ordinary person to enter teaching was a kind of apprenticeship by working as a glorified monitor in the large classes in schools where facilities were poor, discipline severe and rewards and qualifications difficult and harsh to achieve.

He was born at the end of the Victorian Age. Priestley's formative years, therefore, were in the brief period of the relative calm and comfortable Edwardian years (1901–10) which certainly influenced his attitude towards life. He was often to look back on that period as almost a 'golden age' and returned to the years before the First World War again and again in his writings with some **nostalgia** (see Literary Terms).

First World War

He left school at the age of 16 and worked as a junior clerk in a wool office. He was in the Infantry in France for five years during the First World War. He started in the ranks and was later commissioned. He was wounded on three occasions and was always to remember vividly the horrors of his experiences. Interestingly, though, these are never directly referred to in his writings.

After war service

After the First World War, he was awarded a government grant which allowed him to go to Trinity Hall, Cambridge University. There he studied English

Literature, Modern History and Political Science. The course ended in a successful degree.

In 1922 he settled in London. He had already been contributing, with some success, to London and provincial newspapers since he was sixteen. He now met with almost immediate success as a journalist and critic. He was a prolific writer and over the years produced stories, novels, plays and essays. He also gave a series of popular but controversial radio talks during the Second World War for a time on the BBC. These were called *Postscripts* and were broadcast after the Sunday night news bulletins.

Interest in the concept of time

Several of his works concern themselves with the nature of time as well as a preoccupation with the middle classes and social values. He was greatly influenced by the theories of P.D. Ouspensky, especially his book *A New Model of the Universe* which was written in 1931, and by two books written by J.W. Dunne – *An Experiment in Time* (1927) and *The Serial Universe* (1934).

Early successes

The Good Companions (1929), was Priestley's fourth novel. It is one of his first major works and in its rambling jolliness is considered to be one of his best books. It is a highly amusing account of the adventures of a theatrical group on tour. This novel won the James Tait Black Prize – a then coveted award – and firmly established Priestley's already growing reputation. Another outstanding novel is considered to be *Angel Pavement* which was written in 1930. This is seen as a much harsher book and has been described as a story of London life in the **realist school** of writing (see Literary Terms). Two other notable prose works are *Bright Day* (1946) and *Lost Empires* (1965).

General output

He also wrote about 50 plays and dramatic adaptations. The majority of these were published in three volumes

Collected Plays (1948–52). Among the best of his plays
are considered to be *Dangerous Corner* (1932), I *Have
Been Here Before* (1937), *Time and the Conways* (1937)
and *An Inspector Calls*, written in 1945. The last, which
has been described as 'a psychological mystery drama',
had a particularly impressive revival in London in 1999.
He also wrote what might be called some 'experimental
plays' for example, *Johnson over Jordan* (1939) and *They
Came to a City* (1943).

Popularity

Many of his plays have had an enduring popularity and
Time and the Conways, An Inspector Calls and *When We
Are Married* remain an intrinsic part in the repertoire of
both professional and amateur theatrical companies. In
addition there have been film versions of several of his
plays notably: *Dangerous Corner* (1943), *The Good
Companions* (1933 and 1957), *An Inspector Calls* (1954),
Laburnum Grove (1935) and *When We Are Married*
(1943).

**Prose
writings**

A selection of his essays on literature, the arts and travel
appeared in *Essays of Five Decades* published in 1968.
He also published a number of miscellaneous works
ranging from *English Journey* (1934) – which is a
personal account of travels through England – to
collections of his wartime broadcasts in *Britain Speaks*
(1940) and *All England Listened* (1968).

**Time of
contentment**

In 1955 he wrote *Journey Down a Rainbow* in
collaboration with his third wife Jacquetta Hawkes
whom he married in 1953. This describes their travels
in New Mexico.

From two earlier marriages he had five daughters and a
son. His first wife died of cancer in 1925 and he
divorced his second wife.

There have been many autobiographical works such as
Rain Upon Godshill (1939), *Margin Released* (1962) and
Instead of the Trees (1977).

Later
achievements

Naturally, as his life spanned nine decades, he was able to bring a wealth of observation and experience into his writing. He lived through an amazing time of historical upheavals and scientific and technological advances. This often underlined and reinforced his social and political comment. He greatly admired H.G. Wells and liked to see himself as a spokesman of the common person and for common sense. However, he always had difficulty in coming to terms with any particular political party. He stood for parliament as an Independent candidate in the post Second World War election but was unsuccessful. He became a supporter for the Campaign for Nuclear Disarmament (CND) but eventually backed out of it when he felt the organisation was becoming too extreme.

He was a United Kingdom delegate to two UNESCO conferences, Chairman of the British Theatre Conference and was Chairman of the Council on the London Philharmonic Orchestra. He also held the position of Director of the *New Statesman* and *Nation*.

His general
attitude

All in all, he seems to have felt that his sort of social and political ideal was based on compassion. We can see this clearly expressed in the **dénouement** (see Literary Terms) of *An Inspector Calls* and to a lesser extent in *When We Are Married*. His output was huge and he always worked at speed. *An Inspector Calls* was written in one week. It was also said of Priestley that he rarely corrected any of his first drafts.

Above all he will be remembered as a champion for the ordinary man and woman who could make us think about, as well as laugh at, many aspects of our society.

Priestley's general achievement

Many critics have suggested that Priestley is at his best when he is least concerned with openly reforming his audience or being **didactic** (see Literary Terms). This he really achieves in comic pieces such as *Laburnum Grove* and *When We Are Married* or in the wryer humour of *An Inspector Calls* when his gift for portraying ordinary Yorkshire people is given full scope. It is obvious that Priestley thoroughly enjoyed his involvement with such characters and situations – many recalled experiences from his early days in Bradford. The characters become three-dimensional and are down-to-earth and the comedy they give rise to is both bold and forthright.

Most audiences required dramatic entertainment which did not tax them too much but held their attention. However improbable the plot, *When We Are Married* certainly holds our attention, mainly because of the plot and the clash of characters. Much of the **irony** (see Literary Terms) is that the audience knows more of the truth before the main characters do.

Some of Priestley's aims and attitudes

His comedies were written with several aims in mind – to entertain, to show people 'as they are', what motivates them and how they behave in certain circumstances. Whenever possible, even if by **implication** (see Literary Terms) he suggests both a social and political message through his characters and their situations.

Priestley was a dominant force in the theatre of the 1930s onwards. In fact, it was Priestley, along with other writers of the time, who helped to 'break the mould' of the aloof snobbery of the traditional drawing-room **domestic drama** (see Literary Terms). Many of his plays laugh at the pretensions of **provincial** (see Literary Terms) life and the snobbery that goes with this.

Several of his plays are set in the houses of the **nouveau riche** (see Literary Terms). He was also interested in the family unit and, as with *When We Are Married*, some of his plays start with some kind of apparently happy reunion of families or friends. He seems to have been intrigued by the **transience** (see Literary Terms) of the family unit. The family, after all, consists of a group tied together by fate. We may be able to choose our friends but we cannot choose our family!

Some of Priestley's own views

Priestley once wrote: 'The theatrical tradition of our time is a **naturalistic tradition** [see Literary Terms], so I have in the main had to come to terms with it.'

When We Are Married, described as a 'Yorkshire **Farcical Comedy** (see Literary Terms), is a play that has had an enduring popularity, with both professional and amateur companies over the years. It was first produced in London at the St Martin's Theatre in 1938 and moved to the Prince's Theatre in March 1939. When it was revived in London in 1970, the play still had an immediate impact much to the surprise of some critics. Its original runs from 1938–39, made a popular diversion for the audience from the rumblings of the Second World War which was imminent.

It was a great success from the start. Priestley himself said of this play:

> I enjoyed writing this broadly farcical comedy because I had a lot of enjoyment remembering then using various aspects of West Riding life and manners known to me in my boyhood. The plot is nonsensical but the characters and their attitudes and their talk are all authentic ... It was in the earlier part of its run that I had to take over – at twenty-four hours' notice, the part of Henry Ormonroyd, the drunken photographer, and thus did some acting of which I have boasted ever since. (*The Plays of J.B. Priestley*, volume 2, p. x)

Parochialism,
snobbery and
class

The three men of the marriages have, in their different ways, made names for themselves in their local community. Perhaps Albert Parker, alderman, councillor and mill owner is the most objectionable of them all as he is very pompous and self-important (see Commentary). Apparently it is 1908 as we are told the wedding took place in 1883.

It was a world alien in many ways to our own. Queen Victoria's reign, towards the end of which these couples were married, followed by the Edwardian period (1901–10), was a period of growing power and wealth for the country. Many were able to make fortunes as worldwide trade expanded. It was a relatively peaceful time and the rigid class structure made sure that every member of society 'knew their place'. Albert Parker **personifies** (see Literary Terms) the self-made man – comfortably off, assured to the point of arrogance, self-opinionated and brash. We also feel the background influence of the Chapel in this play. The Chapel and its elders could not be questioned – or if they were – it would lead to disgrace or dismissal. This makes the central dilemma of the three couples even more shaming to them than it might today. Yet extremes of wealth and poverty were sharply contrasted with one another. Even middle-class homes had a servant or servants.

This 'cosy' existence was to be shattered by the First World War, but, for the moment it serves well as a background to a possible scandal and the humorous recriminations which turn out to have been unnecessary all along. One of the greatest **ironies** (see Literary Terms) lies in the title of the play which is taken from a well known duet of the time:

When we are married …
– Why what will you do?
– I'll be as sweet as I can be to you;
I will be tender
         – And I will be true
When I am married, sweetheart, to you.

PART TWO

SUMMARIES

GENERAL SUMMARY

Act I   The play opens in the sitting-room of the Helliwells' house. Ruby, the general maid, shows Gerald Forbes into the room. We learn that the Helliwells, with their friends the Parkers and the Soppitts, are just finishing a special high tea. They are celebrating their joint Silver Wedding anniversary (25 years). Nancy Holmes, Joseph Helliwell's niece, is also at the meal. She has been secretly meeting Gerald Forbes with whom she is in love. Gerald was recently appointed organist at the local Chapel but as a 'southerner' his nonchalant behaviour and modern clothes do not meet with the approval of Joseph Helliwell, Albert Parker and Herbert Soppitt who appointed him and Gerald has been summoned to see them.

A photographer from the *Yorkshire Argus*, Henry Ormonroyd, already somewhat the worse for drink, arrives along with a reporter, Fred Dyson. They have been sent to take a photograph of the happy couples for their newspaper. However, as the company has not yet finished their meal, they decide to return to the pub and come back later.

Gerald returns and the women leave the menfolk to deal with him. They find it very difficult to corner Gerald and before they can properly do so, Gerald drops a bombshell. He reveals that on a recent holiday in Wales, he made the acquaintance of a Francis Edwin Beech, a clergyman. He was the priest who married the couples twenty-five years earlier. Beech has subsequently written to Gerald confessing that, although he did not realise it, he was not properly licensed to marry anyone at that time. So, the marriage of the Helliwells, the Parkers and the Soppitts is invalid. This throws everything into disarray.

The men are desperate to hide the truth for fear of ridicule by the local community. However, Mrs Northrop, the charwoman, and a compulsive eavesdropper, has been listening at the door. She is delighted to think that the high and mighty airs of the three couples have been deflated. She will, no doubt, relish passing on the gossip.

Act II   The wives have been deserted by their husbands who have slipped away to their local club to talk the problem through. The women are about to play a card game called Newmarket. Mrs Northrop and Maria Helliwell clash when Maria is trying to sack her. However, as Mrs Northrop gloatingly reveals the information to the women, she puts them into a state of blackmail. That they should learn the news from the charwoman and not their own husbands, is particularly galling. Mrs Northrop eventually leaves, discontented that she has not been paid all she thinks she is due, but exulting in the women's embarrassment.

When the men return, the wives are ready for them and full of righteous indignation. Eventually, they all go into the dining-room to discuss the matter further. There follows a **dialogue** (see Literary Terms) between Ruby and Ormonroyd who has returned even more tipsy than before. Clara Soppitt persuades Ormonroyd to leave.

Lottie Grady arrives and horrifies the wives by revealing that Mrs Northrop has told her the truth about their marriages. They are further alarmed and furious when Lottie tells them she has come to see an old 'gentleman' friend whom she had met some time before in Blackpool. The man had said to her that if he were not married already, he would marry her! She rubs it in further by referring to the women's maiden names and their humble origins.

The man Lottie is referring to turns out to be Joseph Helliwell who, presumably, had made the remark to Lottie in fun. It transpires that not only did Helliwell go on a 'business trip' to Blackpool some time before, but also he was accompanied by Parker and Soppitt.

Before anything can be said further the local Mayor comes in dressed in full regalia representing the Council and Corporation of Cleckleywyke and accompanied by a bevy of reporters. He presents the Helliwells with a gift of a case of fish slices for their silver wedding. In the strained circumstances, all Helliwell can say is: 'I don't like fish'.

Act III Ruby, the maid, is tidying up. Nancy, Helliwell's niece, and Gerald re-appear from the conservatory. We learn that Lottie Grady is still in the house as is Ormonroyd, the photographer, who is now well on the way to getting drunk.

The Parkers and the Soppitts now give vent to their views on marriage and what difference it makes to their relationships if they are *not* married. Lottie repeats that Joseph Helliwell had, in a moment of devilment in Blackpool, told her he would marry her if he were free to do so. Maria Helliwell is naturally upset and makes as if to leave home – much to Lottie's horror.

When Ormonroyd re-appears, much the worse for drink, he greets Lottie as a long lost friend. They reminisce and leave together. Albert Parker suggests that they should all calm down and think of a plan in order to stop the spread of a scandal which would ruin them as well as make them a laughing-stock in the community.

They have managed to find Mrs Northrop and have got her to come back to the Helliwell's again. Mrs

Northrop implies that she will keep her mouth shut if they pay her off. This precipitates an outcry from the couples. Before the problem can be solved the Rev. Clement Mercer arrives. He had already been given the letter that Gerald had been sent by the Rev. Francis Beech in which he had confessed that any marriages he had conducted twenty-five years before were invalid. The Rev. Mercer says that as far as he can see the facts in the letter are true and the couples are *not* legally married.

Ormonroyd returns, a glass of beer in his hand and well on the way to being quite drunk. It is then that Lottie reveals that Ormonroyd has something to tell them that may be of interest. We learn that Ormonroyd was also married twenty-five years before by the same Rev. Beech and in the same circumstances as the Helliwells, the Parkers and the Soppitts!

However, Ormonroyd, who is now separated from his wife, recalls that a Registrar had to attend weddings in the Chapel in those days. As a Registrar was present and signed the marriage certificate they are in fact all legally married after all. With this the couples are reconciled.

DETAILED SUMMARIES

ACT I

PART ONE (PP. 3–5)

The date is 5 September 1908.

The **stage direction** (see Literary Terms) establishes that the owner, Alderman Helliwell, is a good, solid citizen but someone who is **nouveau riche** (see Literary Terms), for 'the room is furnished without taste'. That we meet two of what might be considered minor characters first in the play has some significance. Both Gerald and Ruby, in their own ways, are critical of those who consider themselves to be their superiors.

Ruby is not just a 'flat' conventional stage maid (see Commentary). There is a depth to her character and she possesses common sense as well as a degree of cunning. She makes sure she gets the shilling bribe from Gerald – although we are pretty convinced that she would not give away the secret that she saw Gerald and Nancy together recently one evening.

Consider what you learn about Ruby and Gerald here. We learn that 'they' (the Helliwells, the Parkers and the Soppitts) are still finishing a special high tea. Ruby is rather overwhelmed by the extravagance of it all and she is somewhat scandalised by the fact that they have 'a little brown jug' at the table which means a jug with rum in it to lace their tea with. We learn that Gerald is courting Nancy Holmes, the Helliwells' niece. Gerald asks Ruby to go into the dining-room to tip off Nancy that he is there. It transpires that this special meal is to celebrate the Silver Wedding (25 years) of the three couples.

We also meet, briefly, Mrs Northrop the charwoman, and recognise in her a down-to-earth woman who will not shrink from saying what she thinks. She is described as being aggressive but not without humour.

COMMENT

We have highlighted in the **stage direction** (see Literary Terms) two aspects of the Helliwells and their friends. They are good, solid citizens and, by implication, respected pillars of their community. Secondly, they are wealthy enough to employ a maid and a charwoman with all its suggestion of middle-class comfort and pretensions. However, the keeping of servants would not have been considered unusual in the period in which the play is set (1908).

In addition, Priestley goes out of his way to point out that Gerald does not talk with a **West Riding** (see Literary Terms) accent. This is held against him to some extent, along with his name, Gerald (see what Parker has to say page 18). The prejudice is obviously firmly entrenched and a cause of tension between Gerald and the others. It is as if Gerald, despite his excellent qualifications, cannot be fully accepted because he is a 'southerner'. The Soppitts also do not speak with a Yorkshire accent and they are looked down upon to a certain extent by the Helliwells and the Parkers. After all Joseph Helliwell is an Alderman, Albert Parker is a Councillor whereas Herbert Soppitt is a mere 'Mister'.

Note how Priestley attempts to imitate the Yorkshire accent, especially by using shortened forms of words:– 'o' rum' = of rum; 't'pit' = the pit; 'meself' = myself.

GLOSSARY

slavey an all-purpose servant

give her the tip tell her, tip her off

been pined starved

gassin' gassing – gossiping, talking about

PART TWO (PP. 5–9)

Gerald has been warned by Mrs Northrop of the reason Mr Helliwell has summoned him here. As elders of the Chapel, Mr Helliwell, along with Mr Parker and Mr Soppitt, are dissatisfied with Gerald's reputation and reported behaviour. Although this is mainly gossip exaggerated by prejudice because of Gerald's southern ways, these men do have great influence in the local community.

Nancy comes in and greets Gerald excitedly. They have, we learn, been secretly meeting for some time. Nancy is convinced that her uncle, Joseph Helliwell, would not approve of their relationship. They also comment on

Councillor Parker, whom Nancy describes as 'beastly' and Gerald says he 'loathes him' (p. 6). Nancy warns Gerald that the others have been making remarks and complaining about him and that he should take care. They are about to leave together, when Ormonroyd the photographer and Dyson the reporter from the *Yorkshire Argus*, are shown in. As they learn that they are early and that the special meal has not yet finished, Ormonroyd says that he and Dyson will go off for about half an hour to have some beer back at *The Lion*. Gerald and Nancy hear the Helliwells, the Parkers and the Soppitts approaching, so they slip out through the conservatory.

Examine what you learn about Ormonroyd.

COMMENT   We learn that Gerald is out of favour with Helliwell and that the secret relationship between Nancy and Gerald is a strong one. The disapproving banter of Ormonroyd indicates that Councillor Parker is generally disliked. Nancy has already described him as 'beastly' (p. 6).

We can deduce that the wedding of the three couples took place on 5 September 1883 (p. 9).

GLOSSARY   **tuck-in** a meal, a feast

PART THREE (PP. 9–12)

What do you learn about the difference in character of the three couples?

We meet the three couples for the first time. They appear to enjoy bickering with one another and the give and take of petty argument. The **stage directions** (see Literary Terms) go a long way to show a differentiation between each character. It is clear that Maria Helliwell is determined to sack Mrs Northrop. Her main failing seems to be that she is prepared to stand up for herself which Maria sees as insubordination. As a servant she should know her place and it is not up to the Mrs Northrops of this world to question their masters or show any personal views. It is also implied that Mrs, Northrop drinks too much. However, we do not witness anything much more serious than her drinking the occasional bottle of stout. It is interesting to notice that it is domineering, loud Clara Soppitt who has the most to say about Mrs Northrop here and later in the play – more than her employer Maria Helliwell.

The women reminisce about their wedding day twenty-five years before and comment on how nervous the priest had been when conducting the service. The men, rather tediously, discuss the ups and downs of the animal market, especially sheep sales.

COMMENT

The **stage direction** (see Literary Terms) tells us a great deal about the characters of the three couples (see Commentary). Priestley makes a clear distinction between the Standard, less accented spoken English of Henry Soppitt and Mrs Parker and the broader Yorkshire accents of the others. It may well be that Clara Soppitt is falsifying her manner of speaking because she thinks it may sound more refined.

Helliwell makes a great fuss about his cigars and offers them round. Councillor Parker cannot resist name-dropping in his pompous way with his reference to Sir Harold Watson (p. 11). So, he implies that he is not only an important person, but goes to a Club and mixes with important people.

They then decide to toast one another to celebrate the occasion and Helliwell then rings for the maid.

GLOSSARY

sententious pompous

genteel excessively refined

she likes a drop she is fond of drinking

La Corona make of expensive cigar

complacently with self-satisfaction

He was only like two-pennorth o' copper timid, insignificant

Crossbreeds / Merinos breeds of sheep

Wool Exchange originally a building used as a sheep market for bartering wool and animals

PART FOUR (PP. 12–19)

Note all seems well and full of contentment for the couples here.

They discuss the impudence of servants in general and Mrs Northrop in particular. We notice how fierce and unyielding Clara Soppitt and Albert Parker are in their views. Parker says: 'They're all alike, that class of people' failing to recognise that he probably once belonged to the same class. Annie Helliwell, however, tries to suggest: 'but I suppose they don't know any better'. To which Parker retorts: 'They know a lot better. And what you want to stick up for 'em for, I can't think.'

Ruby brings in a tray of glasses and, unnecessarily, *three* bottles of port. This is another way of Mrs Northrop showing contempt for her 'betters'. She may even be hinting that perhaps they like their drink too much! Helliwell suggests that they should toast the occasion positioned in the places they were in when the original photograph of the wedding group was taken. The toast (p. 15) is 'marriage' – which will turn out shortly to be **ironic** (see Literary Terms).

Nancy returns and says she is going to see a friend –
Muriel Spencer – although we suspect she is really
meeting Gerald.

Maria Helliwell suggests that the women should leave
the men to their Chapel business, and they go back into
the dining-room. Pages 18–19 highlight the prejudices
of the men towards the 'southerner' Gerald. Gerald is
now ushered in by Alderman Joseph Helliwell.

COMMENT   This section focuses on two main issues and prejudices.
The first is tied up with Mrs Northrop and what is
considered her impudence. The view is given that
servants no longer 'know their place' and 'things are not
what they were'. The second is the suspicion of
southerners. Parker is particularly spiteful and Soppitt
supports him in his mocking views and comments.
However, note that Helliwell's objections, although he
does make scornful remarks about Gerald's clothes, are
more practical. These mainly concern the fact that
Gerald's efforts have not matched the promises of his
qualifications and the social 'one-up-man-ship' of their
community. He did not get the village's performance of
the **Messiah** (see Literary Terms) in first which would
have put Cleckleywyke in the spotlight. They are only
interested in the *Messiah* as a status symbol. This also

highlights their hypocrisy. They feel that Gerald should be more sombre and, at least superficially, respectable. We have already noted that Helliwell was impressed by Gerald's qualifications but when Soppitt dares, weakly, to suggest that Gerald's production of the **Messiah** in the end 'was a good one', he is rebuffed by Helliwell: 'by that time who cared?' (p. 19). What they are really concerned about is keeping up appearances which is clearly revealed in Helliwell's question: 'we can't have any carrying on, can we?'. Appearances are all important.

GLOSSARY   **thingummytite**   a fill in word when you cannot remember someone's name

an' no lip   and no answering back

facetiously   in a sly joking manner

plaintively   with complaint

primness   narrowness and intolerance

PART FIVE (PP. 19–30)

The 'interview' with Gerald begins by his being rebuked by Parker for preparing to light a cigarette. Eventually Helliwell comes to the point. He states that Lane End Chapel is the biggest church in a very respectable district and implies that all those associated with it should be equally respectable. Gerald's answers and comments show that he is quite able to hold his own in the face the pomposity and hypocrisy of these self-important men. There is **dramatic irony** (see Literary Terms) in that when Parker tells Gerald has been seen with a girl (or different girls), they do not realise, as the audience does, that she is Nancy, Helliwell's niece. Eventually Helliwell gives Gerald an ultimatum: 'Either behave yourself or get back where you came from.'

Gerald produces some startling information.

It is then that Gerald drops his bombshell. He tells them that he has just been on holiday in North Wales where he made the acquaintance of a parson named the Rev. Beech. When the Rev. Beech learnt that Gerald came from Cleckleywyke, 'he became very excited'. Subsequently, Gerald has received a letter from the Rev. Beech stating that when he conducted marriages twenty-five years before he was not licensed to do so, so any marriage he officiated at was invalid.

Note the reaction to these revelations. The men are stunned when they read the letter which proves that what Gerald has said is true. The first thing that they fear is the reaction of their wives. Then they are afraid of being made a laughing-stock in the eyes of their community. They feel that the information must be kept secret at all costs. Gerald allows them to keep Beech's letter for a while provided it is kept by Soppitt, who has least to lose in the eyes of the community and seems the most trustworthy of the three.

Gerald promises that he will not tell anyone about the letter and its contents. But, of course, he has now turned the tables on the men and they will think twice before challenging Gerald again for fear he would reveal the truth.

The men decide to go to their club to talk over the situation further, leaving Gerald behind.

Mrs Northrop comes in. She has been drinking and, as Gerald suspects, she has been eavesdropping and has heard everything that has been said. Mrs Northrop is exultant. Armed with this information, she can get her own back on the upstart women. The Act ends with Mrs Northrop purposely smashing one of the Helliwells' dishes and convulsed with laughter.

COMMENT   This section is important for many reasons. It highlights some of the differences in character between Alderman Helliwell, Councillor Parker and Mr Soppitt. (see Commentary). In addition the hypocrisy of the men is focused. At all costs they believe, especially

What do we learn further of the characters of Helliwell, Parker and Soppitt?

Helliwell and Parker, that they must preserve the dignity and importance of their positions in the local community and the Chapel. Today, the dilemma might not seem quite so crucial, but we should try to see the events in their historical and social context. The situation gives Priestley the opportunity to bring out the comic tension of what *seems* to be the truth and what actually *is* the truth. Near the end of this section (p. 27) Helliwell and Parker are all over Gerald praising him and his achievements in contrast to what they had been saying in private earlier.

The situation may seem far-fetched, as is the coincidental meeting between the Rev. Beech and Gerald. But this is the stuff of farce where the pompous are ridiculed and the self-important are deflated.

GLOSSARY

remonstrates disapproves
Plain mud just a nobody
gallivanting away gadding about
twaddle nonsense, rubbish
patronizingly condescendingly
culpable negligence guilty of error
Brek break

A *Identify the speaker.*

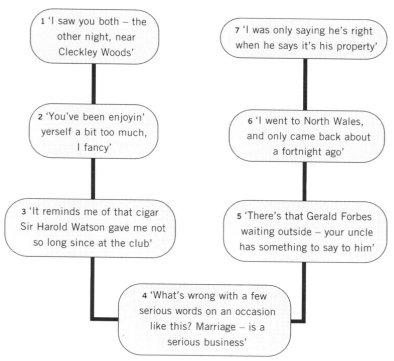

1 'I saw you both – the other night, near Cleckley Woods'

7 'I was only saying he's right when he says it's his property'

2 'You've been enjoyin' yerself a bit too much, I fancy'

6 'I went to North Wales, and only came back about a fortnight ago'

3 'It reminds me of that cigar Sir Harold Watson gave me not so long since at the club'

5 'There's that Gerald Forbes waiting outside – your uncle has something to say to him'

4 'What's wrong with a few serious words on an occasion like this? Marriage – is a serious business'

Check your answers on page 68.

B *Consider these issues.*

a The extent to which the opening stage direction indicates the Helliwells' status.

b Give an assessment of the character of Mrs Northrop.

c What you learn about the differences of character of Alderman Helliwell, Councillor Parker and Herbert Soppitt.

d Outline several examples of prejudice revealed in Act I.

e The reactions of each man to the contents of the letter that Gerald receives from the Rev. Beech.

ACT II

It is the same setting – the Helliwells' drawing-room. Half an hour has passed.

The wives are puzzled as to the whereabouts of their husbands. They thought that perhaps they had just gone outside for a smoke. Ruby has been sent to look for them, without success. However, Ruby does report that Mrs Northrop has been behaving strangely as well as laughing to herself all the time. They then learn, via Ruby and Mrs Northrop, that the menfolk have gone to their club which scandalises the wives as they cannot understand why they have done so on this particularly important evening. When the menfolk return they are given a frosty reception with accusations that the women feel that they have been deserted on this night of nights. The section is full of **irony** (see Literary Terms) as the women still do not know about the invalid marriage.

The men make to go into the dining-room because they have 'summat to talk over'. Left alone the women make further complaints to one another about their husbands and again, ironically, about marriage.

Mrs Northrop enters. She is in a belligerent mood. The women try to be dignified. There is a dispute as to how

How important is it that it is Mrs Northrop who breaks the news? much money she is owed for her work and, in trying to sack her, Maria Helliwell causes Mrs Northrop to be even more insubordinate. It is interesting to note that the bossy Clara Soppitt butts into the argument which, actually, is none of her business. After several dark hints, Mrs Northrop says that she would not want to come back to work for Mrs Helliwell after what she knows about them. She eventually lets it out that they are not legally married.

At first the women disbelieve her. Disgruntled, Mrs Northrop storms out saying that she is still owed five shillings and sixpence.

COMMENT   This passage is interesting from several points of view. It allows the playwright to use a considerable amount of ironic humour. Mrs Northrop, in her challenging way, is given the opportunity to point out that the women, who think themselves so important, have all come from more or less humble backgrounds. She particularly rounds on Maria Helliwell and Clara Soppitt: 'I remember time when you were weighin' out apples an' potatoes in your father's greengrocer's shop, corner o' Park Road, an' a mucky little shop it wor an' all'. When the women at last begin to believe her story, it does not immediately dawn on them that they should somehow prevent Mrs Northrop from spreading the gossip. They let her go and, before they can get her back, it will presumably be too late.

The timing of the play is interesting as the time that passes from the beginning to the end of the play is approximately two and a half hours – the exact time the action of the play takes to run.

GLOSSARY   **barmpot** fool, lunatic

better than a turn at t'Empire more entertaining than a Music Hall performance

sovereign a pre-decimal gold coin which was worth a pound

PART TWO (PP. 37–43)

Note the reactions
of the women in
this section.

Once the wives are convinced that Mrs Northrop is telling the truth, they want to get her back so that they can pay her five shillings and sixpence and plead for her silence.

Dyson, the reporter from the *Yorkshire Argus*, comes back but after some **ironic** exchanges (see Literary Terms), they manage to send him on his way again.

The husbands return from the dining-room and Parker senses that the women now know the truth. Mrs Soppitt immediately unfairly blames Mr Soppitt for all that has gone wrong. She also forbids him to have any of the whisky that Helliwell offers him. However, the hen-pecked husband, possibly for the first time we feel, ignores his wife's orders.

Helliwell's first reaction is to think that Gerald Forbes was the one who told the women the truth about the wedding. He is truly horrified when he learns that it has come from the gossipy Mrs Northrop. Helliwell orders Mr Soppitt, contrary to Soppitt's better judgement, to follow after Mrs Northrop to The Hare and Hounds and to bring her back at all costs.

COMMENT Now they all know about the invalidity of the marriage it is interesting to note the various reactions of the characters. Behind all the decisions taken at this stage remains the fear of what the wider community will think of them if their secret is revealed.

GLOSSARY **gormless** idiotic
tap-room a bar
pop off (slang) go away
you might just as well play it on Town Hall chimes you might just as well shout it out all round the town for all to hear

PART THREE (PP. 43–6)

The couples now air some honest views about one another.

The couples now confront one another. There is great play, especially from the men, about what it feels like *not* to be married after all. There is a strange sense of relief. It also gives the playwright the opportunity for a great deal of wry humour. We have the feeling that the men feel rather liberated. They are no longer tied to the women so, they can no longer dominate or subdue them.

COMMENT This section is riddled with humour and **irony** (see Literary Terms) and recriminations. The women blame the men for what has happened which is really unjustified and inconsiderate. But, apparently, a man can never get things right and this latest gaffe proves the women right! Eventually they all end up in the dining-room in an attempt to talk things through and try and sort things out.

Pick out the various examples of humour in this passage.

GLOSSARY **fatuous** foolish
ructions arguments
fratchin' rowing

PART FOUR (PP. 46–52)

Suggest what we learn further here about Ruby's character.

There now follows a **dialogue** (see Literary Terms) between Ruby, the maid, and Ormonroyd the photographer from the *Yorkshire Argus*. He is the worse for drink ('very ripe', p. 47). He helps himself to a cigar. He has decided that he would like to take a photograph of the couples in exactly the same positions they were in the original wedding photograph. Once he has set up his camera and temporarily posed Ruby so that he can line up his camera correctly, he deftly helps himself to a glass of whisky. He is getting more and more mellow and starts to become sentimental especially about his own failed marriage. Ruby starts to recite a poem to him that she learnt at school. Ormonroyd has turned his back to her. Before Ruby can finish the final line, Clara enters and Ruby slips out. When he turns round therefore, Ormonroyd is surprised to find himself facing the intimidating Clara. Annie comes in and, flustered, Ormonroyd leaves.

COMMENT   This passage amusingly focuses on Ruby and Ormonroyd. The key information that we learn is that Ormonroyd's wife has left him. She now runs a boarding house in Torquay. This gives him the opportunity to ridicule southerners. He says of

Torquay: 'a favourite all-year-round resort of many delicate and refined persons of genteel society. In other words, it's a damned miserable hole'.

GLOSSARY   **very ripe** drunk
                        bit tiddly drunk
                        squiffy drunk
                        soft pitiable
                        sceptically doubtfully

PART FIVE (PP. 53–9)

The arrival of Lottie Grady adds a complication to the plot.

The three women are now on stage when we hear the doorbell ring. Ruby comes in and tells them there is an unknown woman at the door. Ruby is rather horrified as the woman is heavily made up and she suspects she has dyed hair. Lottie Grady is ushered in. She shocks the women by pointedly referring to them by their maiden names. Lottie reveals that her friend, Mrs Northrop, has revealed the truth of the invalid marriage to her when she saw her just before at *The Hare and Hounds*.

It transpires that Lottie had met 'and had a good time' with Helliwell, Parker and Soppitt when the men had been on a business trip to Blackpool some time before. It turns out that 'one gentleman friend' had said several times that if he had not been married already he would marry Lottie. It was obviously said in a moment of fun, but the women are disgusted and take it seriously. When the men return, it turns out that the 'gentleman friend' is Alderman Helliwell. He had made the remark about marrying Lottie as a light-hearted joke. Now that Lottie has learnt of his present predicament she says she wants to hold him to his offer!

Before anything further can be said, the arrival of the Rev. Mercer interrupts the proceedings. The situation becomes confused as the Rev. Mercer does not really know what is going on. The final straw is the arrival of the Mayor with reporters bearing a gift to the Helliwells from the Council and Corporation of Cleckleywyke.

COMMENT   Much of the humour in this section is caused largely because the audience and the main characters know more than some of the other characters about what is going on. The contrast between the three 'establishment' women and the flighty Lottie is obvious. Although appearances can be deceptive it can work both ways. Lottie's appearance – dyed hair and heavy make-up – indicate a 'loose' woman as judged by Ruby and the three women. Yet the three women with their conventional and upright appearance and behaviour are not what they seem. Confronted by Lottie they fall back on their dignity – dignity, which in the circumstances, makes them look rather ridiculous.

By the end of Act II, everything seems to be getting out of hand and we are put into a mood of anticipation wondering how, if at all, everything can work out for the good.

GLOSSARY   **broadminded** tolerant
reminiscently recalling with fondness
vehemently violently

Identify the speaker.

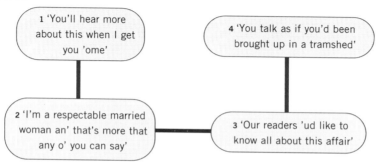

1 'You'll hear more about this when I get you 'ome'

4 'You talk as if you'd been brought up in a tramshed'

2 'I'm a respectable married woman an' that's more that any o' you can say'

3 'Our readers 'ud like to know all about this affair'

Identify the person 'to whom' this comment refers.

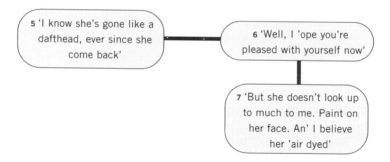

5 'I know she's gone like a dafthead, ever since she come back'

6 'Well, I 'ope you're pleased with yourself now'

7 'But she doesn't look up to much to me. Paint on her face. An' I believe her 'air dyed'

Check your answers on page 68.

 Consider these issues.

a The dialogue between the three women and Mrs Northrop. How do the revelations concerning the marriage gradually sink in?

b Any differentiation in the characters of Maria, Annie and Clara.

c What more you learn of Ruby's character from her conversation with Ormonroyd.

d How the arrival of Lottie Grady affects the course of the play.

ACT III

PART ONE (PP. 60–5)

The setting is the same – the Helliwells' dining-room. It is about a quarter of an hour after the end of Act II. Ruby is tidying up the room when Nancy and Gerald arrive back together. Herbert Soppitt and Annie Parker come in from the garden and catch Nancy and Gerald in a passionate embrace. Nancy admits to them that she is frightened to tell her uncle, Joseph Helliwell, about her romance because he might have objections. Annie shows a sympathetic side to her nature: 'Why don't you go outside and say good night properly? You're only young once'.

Herbert reminds Annie that years ago, before he was married to Clara, he had rather a soft spot for Annie and she reminds him about the choir outing they went on together when he first came to Cleckleywyke. Clara Soppitt comes on stage and sees her husband has his arm round Annie Parker. She momentarily shows jealousy. After all the three men *had* been on the business jaunt to Blackpool and perhaps he cannot be trusted.

The hen-pecked husband revolts. Annie leaves and Clara orders her husband to go home as she feels he cannot really do much more to help, or so she says. However, Herbert refuses and they both end up slapping each other across the face. Herbert now takes control of the situation and Clara is made to submit.

COMMENT The opportunity now arises for the characters to reveal themselves in their true colours: how they really are and how they really feel. Herbert Soppitt illustrates well here the saying 'even a worm will turn'. When Councillor Parker returns he accuses Soppitt of drinking too much. On the more constructive side, it is Parker who now suggests that instead of everyone getting so worked up about the situation, it would be better if the six of them sat down together and tried to work the problem out calmly.

GLOSSARY   **pantymime** pantomime
            'anky-panky deceit, sly cheating
            argy-bargy argument

PART TWO (PP. 65–71)

Albert Parker faces some home truths.   Albert Parker now attempts to justify his achievements to Annie. In a litany of self-praise he reaches what is described as 'a dreamy ecstasy of complacency' (p. 67). He finally speaks to her 'with immense patronage' (p. 67). Annie bides her time apparently submissive. When Albert reaches the peak of self-satisfaction and self-congratulation, Annie turns the tables on him. She says she would not want to marry him now even if she were given the opportunity: 'You see, Albert, after twenty-five years of it, perhaps, I've had enough'. Albert is amazed and falls into the trap of asking Annie what she sees wrong with him. She comes straight to the point, he is: 'selfish', 'conceited', 'stingy', 'dull and dreary'. Albert is absolutely flabbergasted and even more hurt when both Clara Soppitt and Lottie Grady, who come in shortly, support Annie's view as to Albert's stinginess.

COMMENT   It is now time for Albert Parker to learn how others see him. Annie has been the apparently submissive wife for twenty-five years and has stuck by him 'for better or for worse'. Now that the shackles of the marriage vows seem to be removed, she can vent her true feelings. Above all, Annie would like to enjoy herself for once, 'have a bit of fun' as she puts it.

GLOSSARY   **complacently** with self-satisfaction
            demurely modestly
            patronizing superior / self-important

> scrimped eked things out
> getting your hand down putting his hand in his pocket to give money
> I'll give 'em jip I'll deal with them harshly

PART THREE (PP. 71–5)

Joseph Helliwell and Lottie are briefly alone together on the stage. Helliwell tries to pass off his past adventure with her in Blackpool as 'only a bit of fun'. Lottie turns on him saying that therefore she presumably was being used and made fun of.

Maria Helliwell is on the verge of leaving her husband.

Maria comes in 'dressed to go out'. She says she is leaving and going to stay at her mother's. She then turns on Lottie and says she hopes she will enjoy running the house. Maria throws the house keys and the housekeeping account books in disgust on the settee. She also points out that she has left some clothes that need darning and mending. With that she storms out. Lottie has already protested and Joseph Helliwell is mortified and follows after Maria.

Ormonroyd enters and greets Lottie like a long lost friend. Ormonroyd by this time is more than a little fuddled with drink and he and Lottie get into a very muddled and complicated conversation. Eventually they start singing together with Lottie playing the piano. In the midst of this, Helliwell, Parker and Soppitt return. Lottie helps Ormonroyd from the room with Helliwell instructing him that he should go home.

COMMENT   Now it is Joseph Helliwell's turn to face the truth. As Maria sees it, or chooses to see it, Joseph has ruined everything by his secret association with Lottie. We realise that the last thing Lottie wants is to take over the running of a house and 'settle down' as a submissive housewife!

GLOSSARY   **rumpus** uproar
Liberty 'All (Liberty Hall) free house for all
Chin-chin (slang) good-bye
the Talbot name of a public house
Duke of Wellington's – the dirty Thirty-Thirds a vulgar nickname for the Duke of Wellington's regiment

PART FOUR (PP. 75–9)

The three wives enter all dressed ready to go out. Maria confronts Joseph Helliwell and asks him point blank whether he loves her. Helliwell is overcome with embarrassment. He admits that he does love her. The three women sit down and Parker suggests that they should all discuss things instead of going round and round in circles arguing with one another. Before they can go any further, Mrs Northrop re-appears. Helliwell tells her she is not welcome. After they all get very heated, and before anything constructive can be achieved, the Rev. Mercer arrives on the scene.

During all this Ruby looks in twice to say that Ormonroyd has fallen asleep by the phone and when she tells him to go home, he says that this *is* his home! The Rev. Mercer rebukes Mrs Northrop for drinking and makes her promise him that she will say nothing

Part four continued

about what she has witnessed that evening. Contrite, Mrs Northrop agrees.

The play comes to a climax. The Rev. Mercer says that he has studied the Rev. Beech's letter. We think, with the couples, that he will say the letter is a fake, but to their dismay he states that in his opinion, the letter is genuine and so is the information it contains.

Helliwell insults the Rev. Mercer who leaves angrily. However, he does return the Rev. Beech's letter.

COMMENT The play is now reaching its **dénouement** (see Literary Terms). Nothing has been achieved. The couples are apparently unmarried; Lottie is a complication; the photographer is in almost a drunken stupor and Helliwell has upset the Rev. Mercer again. So they are back virtually where they started. What has been achieved is that many things have been aired and admitted which may lead to a greater understanding.

GLOSSARY **crestfallen** dispirited
like a – gurt lion of a man a man worth looking up to
quavering trembling
audacity bravery

PART FIVE (PP. 79–84)

The Helliwells, the Parkers and the Soppitts decide that they really must sort things out. Before they can do more, Ormonroyd wanders in carrying a large glass of beer. When Lottie Grady comes in Clara Soppitt attacks her verbally but Ormonroyd comes to the rescue. There seems to be wisdom in his drunken mellowness:

> We're all in the same boat. We all come 'ere and we don't know why. We all go in our turn and we don't know where. If you are a bit better off, be thankful … What I say is this – we're all human, aren't we?

Ormonroyd having warned Parker that, as he works for a newspaper he has the power of the Press behind him, is immediately told by Ruby that she has just taken a phone call which said he had been sacked.

Ormonroyd has the key to the solution of the dilemma.

Lottie tries to cheer him up and then tells the assembled company that Ormonroyd has something to tell them. It turns out that he was also married twenty-five years ago in the same Chapel by the same priest. Ormonroyd's wife left him and presumably Ormonroyd hoped to make the break official. When Ormonroyd examined his marriage certificate, he noticed that it was also signed by the Registrar as well as the unqualified Rev. Beech. The Registrar's signature was sufficient to make the marriage legal. So, all along the couples had been properly married! Their reaction is, as even Parker puts it, 'to have some fun'.

The play ends on a jolly note. Ormonroyd takes the posed photograph after all. As his old-fashioned flash explodes, Ruby comes in at that moment carrying a tray. The flash surprises her and she drops the tray and its contents on the floor.

COMMENT

Although the **dénouement** (see Literary Terms) may seem contrived, the nature of the play, 'a Yorkshire farcical comedy', permits us to accept the events and the happy ending. Today, we tend to be used to a greater realism and endings of plays either leave a final conclusion to our imagination or end unhappily. We would also not feel the same sense of shock or shame that these couples feel when they discover they have been living together for twenty-five years unmarried.

At the end of the play Helliwell has mellowed somewhat and even Parker is prepared to enjoy himself for once. Perhaps Maria Helliwell sums up the lesson they have learnt best when she says to her husband:

> We'll all have to make the best of each other. But then, perhaps it's what we're here for.

GLOSSARY

game o' solo a card game

there's summat a bit off 'ere there's something not quite right here

A *Identify the speaker.*

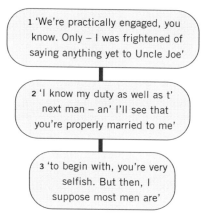

1 'We're practically engaged, you know. Only – I was frightened of saying anything yet to Uncle Joe'

2 'I know my duty as well as t' next man – an' I'll see that you're properly married to me'

3 'to begin with, you're very selfish. But then, I suppose most men are'

Identify the person(s) 'to whom' this comment refers.

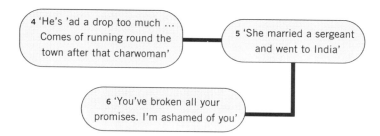

4 'He's 'ad a drop too much ... Comes of running round the town after that charwoman'

5 'She married a sergeant and went to India'

6 'You've broken all your promises. I'm ashamed of you'

Check your answers on page 68.

 B *Consider these issues.*

a What you learn further about Councillor Parker in Act III.

b How the news about the marriage alters the relationship between each couple.

c At the end of the play what we gather the husbands have learnt from their experiences.

PART THREE

COMMENTARY

THEMES

SOCIAL COMMENT

Write down examples of social pretensions revealed in the play.

In *When We Are Married* J.B. Priestley presents to the audience social comment through the attitudes and behaviour of many of the characters. This is clearly seen in the reactions of the husbands, and their wives, to the revelation that they are not legally married when they think they have been wed for twenty-five years. Their horror is compounded by the thought that they will be held to ridicule in their community. Helliwell has reached the august rank of an Alderman; Parker is a Councillor and these trappings of authority and respect are now in danger of being stripped from them. In addition, along with Soppitt, they are respected elders of the church and believe they stand for rectitude and good example.

Likewise, their wives greet the news with apprehension. We gather that they have risen from reasonably humble backgrounds and now their social position is in jeopardy. In addition they are embarrassed about what the servants will think. In fact, their reactions are entirely informed by what they see as social disaster.

SOCIAL ATTITUDES

Consider the relationship between servants and their employers.

The play is set at a time (1905) when it was customary for people to have servants. In the Helliwells' household they have a resident maid of all work, Ruby, and a visiting charwoman, Mrs Northrop. The women's attitudes towards these two are interesting and informative. Mrs Northrop is a woman who does not mind speaking her mind and therefore is disliked by

Maria Helliwell – heavily supported by Clara Soppitt. Maria is determined to sack her for what she sees as insubordination. However, Ruby, who appears more dutiful and submissive, is seen as a 'treasure'. In fact, we the audience, see quite clearly that Ruby is quite incisive in her dealings with people and presumably knows her place only to keep her job and the atmosphere sweet. As she is in no way a nuisance, Maria Helliwell looks upon her with approval.

MARRIAGE, RELATIONSHIPS, LOVE

Think about the different relationships between the various couples.   Marriage is obviously central to the title of this play. Unlike the romantic love we see between Nancy and Gerald, and hinted at about Ruby and her boyfriend 'the milkman's lad', the love between the older couples is seen more as a companionship to which they have become used. It is no more than a status symbol in a society that demands respectability. When the Helliwells, the Parkers and the Soppitts believe that they have not been legally married after all, Priestley has the opportunity to reveal how they really feel and have felt about one another. The revelations turn out to be enough to clear the air and, in the end, this new found honesty makes the relationships all the stronger.

SNOBBERY AND PAROCHIALISM

Consider how pretensions and prejudice bring out humour.   There are several glaring examples of snobbery and parochialism in the play. To a great extent, they are an intricate part of the comic strands in the play. Alderman Helliwell and Councillor Parker come over as self-made, self-centred and pompous men who are ripe for some kind of comic downfall (see Characters).

Their wives bathe in their glory and achievements and obviously consider themselves to be a cut above others in their community. The last thing they want to be reminded of is their humble origins which Mrs Northrop, and later Lottie Grady, delight in pointing out to them.

There is also the prejudice towards 'southerners' which is emphasised here towards Gerald. This is especially seen in the attitudes of Alderman Helliwell and Councillor Parker. Where appearances are so laughably important to these men, they judge Gerald by his 'la di dah' accent and his clothes. They also assume that as local gossip has it that Gerald has been seen with an unnamed local girl, he cannot be honourable.

In fact, of course, Nancy realises that as things stand at the beginning of the play, her uncle, James Helliwell, is unlikely to approve of her liaison with Gerald. The 'north/south' hostility raises its head again later in the play when Henry Ormonroyd says that when his wife left him she went to run a boarding-house in Torquay which he describes as 'a damned miserable hole' because it 'is a favourite all-year-round resort of many delicate and refined persons of genteel society' (p. 49).

OTHER ISSUES

There is also a hint at the fact that the superficiality in the main characters is to do with inter-village rivalry. They are, for example, not interested in the annual performance of the *Messiah* (see Literary Terms) that their Chapel puts on for its own sake, but only because it should be performed with great show and be the first one to be put on in the winter season so as to steal the thunder from other local village Chapels.

Along with this goes the suggestion of following the puritanical work ethic. We see this especially in the mean and overbearing Councillor Parker. Life should be serious with work being uppermost. It is no wonder that his wife laments that she 'wants some fun' in her life!

With this goes the belief that each person has an allotted place in the hierarchy – despite the fact that the Helliwells, Parkers and Soppitts of this world are upstarts. Servants should do as they are told and be submissive. They should not have minds of their own. Councillor Parker makes this view clear about his mill-workers as well 'We have the same trouble at mill. Don't know when they are well off. Idle, that's what they are – bone idle!' (p. 13).

STRUCTURE

Look at the moments when the audience has more information than the characters on stage.

The play follows the conventional three act format. It is so structured that we meet minor characters to begin with and what they say makes us anticipate the arrival of the main characters. The audience wonders what they will be like because Ruby and Gerald have already hinted at what they think of the Helliwells, the Parkers and the Soppitts.

The stage directions are an integral part of the play and help us in reading the play to picture the setting and context of the action as well as how the characters should look and behave.

The playwright keeps the play within what are called 'the three unities'. These unities are of time, place and action. Traditionally a play was meant to be constructed around these unities: events should take place at the same pace as the action on stage (i.e. over one evening) – this is the unity of time; events should take place in one place/setting – this is the unity of place; and events should focus on one main storyline/action – this is the unity of action. In *When we are Married* the setting of the play throughout is the Helliwell's dining-room and the action of the comedy is focused on one main issue (whether the three couples are legally married or not).

Make a plan of when the main characters are on stage and who with.

Priestley is very clever in the way he uses his characters. There is quite a subtlety as to who is on stage at a particular time and how he arranges for the characters to be on or off stage at certain points in the play. We are introduced to three main characters at the beginning of the play and their circumstances, through the comments of Ruby, Gerald and Nancy as well as the stage set. This prepares the audience for what to expect. Perhaps they will or will not live up to the comments made before they appear.

The intervention of Lottie Grady 'out of the blue' redirects the action and the comic potential of the situation. Similarly, Henry Ormonroyd's appearances, as well as Fred Dyson's, add to the movement of the **dialogue** (see Literary terms) and action.

The action and the passage of time in the play are 'realistic' but obviously the events are exaggerated for comic effect. The characters of Helliwell, Parker, Soppitt and their wives are purposely allowed to be magnified almost to the point of caricature, so that their apparent downfall and deflation will make them seem all the more ludicrous. That characters whom they despise, or suspect, such as Gerald and Mrs Northrop bring about this 'downfall' is all the more telling. Likewise, it is the somewhat disreputable, drunken photographer from the *Yorkshire Argus*, Henry Ormonroyd, who brings about the resolution of the plot.

As in all well-written plays and novels, at the end of the comedy we have learnt a great deal more about the characters and what motivates them. We feel that they

have come to know more about themselves and others
and are to some extent changed, if not enlightened.

> MARIA: We'll all have to make the best of each other. But
> then, perhaps it's what we're here for.
>
> ...
>
> PARKER: Well, we had better see if we can have some of this
> fun of yours you talk about.

CHARACTERS

ALDERMAN JOSEPH HELLIWELL, MARIA HELLIWELL, HIS WIFE

Alderman Joseph Helliwell is a prosperous businessman
who, we feel, has 'come up in the world'. He is proud of
his position in his local community as an Alderman and
an elder of the Chapel. He is described in the stage
direction (p. 9), along with his wife, Maria, as 'high-
coloured, rather bouncing, rather pompous, very pleased
with themselves'. They are the hosts and doing the
entertaining for this special anniversary. They are all
described as being 'obviously crammed with high tea'.
They both have strong Yorkshire accents. We later
learn that Helliwell had arranged for the *Yorkshire Argus*
to record the special event of the silver wedding the
publicity of which will no doubt be good for his local
image.

self-assured
overbearing
self-satisfied

Helliwell at this stage in the play is indulging in
generosity to his guests but we feel it is all in the cause
of his own self-gratification. He bickers with his wife
easily but usually gives in to keep the peace (see p. 10).
Like all people assured of their superiority, although
inwardly insecure, he is quite quick to find fault in
others. He mocks the Rev. Beech for his squint and his
nervousness; he agrees with Councillor Parker that
Gerald is bringing disrepute on the respectability of the
Chapel, but Helliwell is, at least, prepared to give
Gerald another chance.

When Gerald eventually gives them the news that their marriage is invalid, Helliwell turns into an ingratiating friend towards Gerald begging him to forget any hard words he may have said to him and showering him with cigars. In fact, Helliwell, along with the other men, is quite ineffectual in coping with the situation. We realise with some amusement, that he is rather afraid of the way their wives will react.

forceful
very aware

Maria, later, says to Councillor Parker about her husband: 'If you'd had twenty-five years of him, you wouldn't talk about might (be married to him)'. To which Helliwell answers back, hurt: "Ere, steady on – with your *twenty-five years of 'im*! Talking about me as if I were a dose o' typhoid fever'.

When the complication with Lottie Grady arises, Maria turns the tables on Joseph Helliwell and actually subdues this man of substance threatening to leave him. He is horrified. We can imagine that Helliwell made the 'promise' to Lottie only as a sop to his own pride believing full well that in any case he was married, so the offer had no real value. So he has been caught out by his own bravado. We know he certainly would not have behaved like that if his wife had been anywhere near. So, in a way, there is some cowardice beneath his self-assured exterior.

Maria Helliwell turns out to be quite a forceful character – not the submissive wife by any means now she has her opportunity to put her foot down. But at the very end of the play they are reconciled and we feel that perhaps their relationship is on a surer footing as a result of their experiences.

COUNCILLOR ALBERT PARKER, ANNIE PARKER

Councillor Albert Parker is generally rather an unpleasant, brash, uncaring man. He revels in his

own importance and apparently delights in sneering at those he sees at a disadvantage. He values his position in his community and in order to preserve his superiority is prepared to belittle others. See what he says about Gerald on pages 18–19. He also cannot resist 'name-dropping' when he refers to 'Sir Harold Watson … at the club' (p. 11).

He is particularly objectionable in the confrontation between the men and Gerald (pp. 20–2). He is also quick to 'pull rank' at the beginning of that interview. When Gerald, (p. 20), refers to him as 'Mr Parker', Parker is very quick to say:

Albert is:

unpleasant

unsympathetic

(*with dignity*): Councillor Parker. (*Pointing*) Alderman Helliwell. Councillor Parker. Mr Soppitt. –

Annie is :

kind

thoughtful

In this he even squashes Herbert Soppitt by pointing out he is only a Mr.

not submissive

Later in the play he receives a bitter revelation of what others really feel he is like. Whereas the other characters speak in a broad Yorkshire accent, Herbert Soppitt and Annie Parker 'talk a rather genteel ordinary English'.

Albert is widely

disliked by others

outside his circle of

associates and

friends.

His wife, Annie, when we first meet her, is described as 'a hopeful kind of woman'. She gives the impression of being kind and thoughtful but totally dominated by her husband. It is Annie who shows kindness towards Nancy and Gerald (p. 61) and if you examine her remarks and comments throughout the play, we see that she tries to look on the bright side of things.

Annie has a mild

and likeable

character.

At long last, she gives her husband as good as she gets when he patronizingly tells her not to worry about their not being married. He will sort it all out and put it all straight.(pp. 65–9). At the climax of this section, Annie rounds on her husband and tells him, in no uncertain terms, that she has had enough of putting up with him.

In addition she tells him he is 'selfish', 'conceited', 'stingy', 'dull and dreary'. She tells him she 'wants some fun' before 'she is an old woman'. Parker is further taken aback when Lottie comes in and says she thinks he looks 'stingy' as well. Yet, the result of all this is that when the problem of the marriage is solved at the end of Act Three, Parker seems to have learnt his lesson and some of the truth about himself (p. 83):

> PARKER: Well, that beats me. I've always seemed to myself as an exciting sort of chap. (*To Annie*) Anyhow, stingy or whatever I am, I'm still your husband.
>
> ANNIE: So it looks as if I'll have to make the best of you.

There is a slight change here from how he was seen at the beginning of the play when Nancy describes Parker as 'beastly' and recognises that Gerald 'loathes' him. Overall, Ormonroyd sums up Parker's reputation succinctly: 'Every time he opens his mouth at the Town Hall, he puts his foot in it, so they call him "the foot and mouth disease" ' (p. 8).

HERBERT SOPPITT, CLARA SOPPITT

Of the three men, Herbert Soppitt comes over as the most likeable. He is much more accommodating and reasonable and, although he joins with Parker in laughing at Gerald's 'La-di-dah' ways (p. 18), the stage direction indicates that it is because 'he has a sense of humour'. Parker's criticisms and comments are, on the other hand, intentionally malicious. There is no malice in Soppitt and if you look carefully at what he has to say, he is usually trying to smooth things over. In the interview with Gerald he tries to be the appeaser, without much apparent success.

Clara is described in the stage directions as 'a noisy woman'. She enjoys butting in with her comments and observations. When Mrs Helliwell is scolding

Herbert is:
the most likeable
of the three men,
not malicious

Clara is:
brash but
eventually
subdued

Mrs Northrop, Clara adds comments as well despite the fact that the problem has nothing to do with her at all. Eventually, Herbert Soppitt turns on his wife, they even come to blows, but she is subdued by her husband in the end (pp. 62–3). Herbert Soppitt at long last asserts his authority over his shrew of a wife. At the end of the play it is quite clear who is in charge (p. 83):

SOPPITT: we won't be [happy] if you don't drop that tone of voice. I don't like it.

CLARA: Yes, Herbert.

RUBY BIRTLE

Ruby is the Helliwell's resident maid-of-all-work. One of her main tasks is to answer the front door. In doing this she is in a position to 'vet' visitors before they are brought in and introduced. This she clearly does with someone whom she thinks is a stranger such as Lottie Grady.

Consider how
Ruby interacts
with other
characters
throughout the
play.

She belongs to a long line of cheeky but intelligent servants. She is more intelligent than she is given credit for and possibly more so than her employers and their friends. This helps to throw a perspective on the pretensions of the Helliwells, the Parkers and the Soppitts. She comes alive through her manner of forthright speech and attitude as a person in her own right. We feel that she is reliable and loyal. Her sense of humour is limited as she does not fully appreciate the **ironies** (see Literary Terms) in her conversations with Gerald and Ormonroyd (pp. 3–5 and pp. 47–52). Above all Ruby is cheerful, optimistic and likeable. She is, at times, quite prepared to say what she thinks (though, cleverly not to her employers, the Helliwells): 'You've been neglectin' yerself' (p. 48); 'Too much liftin' o' t'elbow' (p. 48); 'Yer wife doesn't seem to tak much interest in yer' (p. 49).

MRS NORTHROP

A down-to-earth woman who speaks her mind. She is described by Priestley as 'an aggressive but humorous working-woman of about fifty'. She is later described by Maria Helliwell as her charwoman. She is also a somewhat rebellious woman, a gossip who likes a drink. She is quite prepared to stand up for herself against the other women when accused of stealing (which is obviously false), and not doing her job properly. She takes a moral stance when she overhears that the couples are apparently not legally married. This gives her the opportunity to show an amusing righteousness – after all she has always been proud enough to recognise that the Helliwells, the Parkers and the Soppitts were never really superior in their origins to her. She is an inveterate eavesdropper and quite prepared to speak her mind: 'They've got it in for you' (p. 5); 'To 'ell with 'em!' (p. 5).

When Clara Soppitt joins in Maria's criticisms she is ready to stand up for herself and turn on Clara: 'Who's asking you to pass remarks?' (p. 35). Even though the Rev. Mercer chides her into an apology, she still has the last word: '(I'm) worth all you lot put together' (p. 78).

OTHER CHARACTERS

Henry Ormonroyd
Dissolute but cheerful and observant.

Ormonroyd, the photographer from the *Yorkshire Argus*, is a drunken reprobate. He carries an old fashioned camera and is described as having a 'beery dignity' (p. 7). He has a large drooping moustache and is not without a sense of humour. He excels in small talk, for example with Gerald Forbes (p. 7) and Ruby (pp. 47–52). By the time he is really the worse for drink he has a very convoluted and muddled conversation with Lottie Grady (pp. 73–5). In the end, it is Ormonroyd who helps solve the riddle concerning the marriages.

Lottie Grady
The 'disrupter'.

Lottie Grady's appearance on the scene causes further disruption to the situation. When Ruby tells Maria and the others that there is a woman at the door she says of Lottie:

> RUBY: ... she doesn't look up to much to me. Paint on her face. An' I believe her 'air's dyed.
> *The three women look at each other.*
> CLARA: (primly): We don't want that sort o' woman here, Maria.

So Lottie is condemned by her appearance as a 'loose woman'. When it turns out that Joseph Helliwell had flirted with her in Blackpool, Maria is so incensed she threatens to leave home.

Lottie's purpose in the play is mainly twofold. She throws the falseness of the other women's pose of superiority into relief and, as a friend of Ormonroyd, she is able to help in the unravelling of the dilemma of the play.

Gerald Forbes and Nancy Holmes

Gerald, the recently appointed organist at Lane End Chapel, is a southerner. He is a cultured young man but is looked on with suspicion by the Yorkshire 'establishment'. We notice that he can hold his own in his interview with Helliwell, Parker and Soppitt in Act I. He is the instrument of the confusion in the play when he produces the letter from the Rev. Beech.

Nancy Holmes is Joseph Helliwell's niece. She has felt forced to be deceptive about her relationship and love for Gerald because of her uncle's prejudices. We see her deception in practice when she pretends she is going to see a certain Muriel Spencer (p. 17) when she is really meeting Gerald, we suspect.

The only other characters we meet are the Rev. Mercer whose role is minimal and the Mayor of Cleckleywyke who appears briefly at the end of Act II.

Priestley highlights, as in the best of comedy, some of
the everlasting faults of mankind, such as snobbery,
pomposity, self-satisfaction, self-aggrandisement and
self-delusion. Thus he is concerned with the eternal
follies of human beings.

The realism of The play presents us, through its setting and language,
the dialogue a realistic insight into the characters and their
and setting surroundings. By his spelling Priestley attempts to
imitate a Yorkshire accent except in the cases of
Herbert Soppitt and Annie Parker who speak 'a rather
genteel ordinary English'. In addition, from the way the
language is written down, we assume that Gerald, and
possibly Nancy, do not speak with a Northern accent.
He also uses some Northern dialect words to give
authenticity to his speakers. All this helps to make the
characters recognisable through **dialogue** (see Literary
Terms), action and description.

The **stage directions** (see Literary Terms), both long
and short, give us excellent impressions as to how the
characters look and how they should behave and react.

The setting, as described at the beginning of Act I, is
the same throughout the play. This gives us a clear
indication as to the position of the Helliwells with the
suggestion that they do not have particularly good taste.

Methods of Priestley's humour is mainly achieved through **dramatic**
humour **irony** (see Literary Terms). We also note that he uses
social awareness, or sometimes a lack of it, to highlight
the pomposity or self-delusion of some characters – this
is especially seen in the Helliwells, the Parkers and the
Soppitts. Also he puts characters of different class or
temperament alongside one another – e.g. Gerald and
Ruby; Lottie and the other women; Ruby and the
inebriated Ormonroyd. All the while we should
examine the position and knowledge of the audience in
relation to the characters and the action. It is also useful

to consider how far we sympathise with a character (or not) and why. For example, when Herbert Soppitt eventually turns on his wife, Clara, we probably might look upon him favourably. Perhaps we really feel we would just have liked to have done that. Again, we may feel for Lottie Grady just because the other women are prejudiced against her initially because of her appearance.

Humour here is mainly of situation, character and verbal use. By these means, Priestley is able to convince us momentarily that the ludicrous situation is actually capable of taking place.

PART FOUR

STUDY SKILLS

HOW TO USE QUOTATIONS

One of the secrets of success in writing essays is the way you use quotations. There are five basic principles:
- Put inverted commas at the beginning and end of the quotation
- Write the quotation exactly as it appears in the original
- Do not use a quotation that repeats what you have just written
- Use the quotation so that it fits into your sentence
- Keep the quotation as short as possible

Quotations should be used to develop the line of thought in your essays.

Your comment should not duplicate what is in your quotation. For example:

Ruby tells Maria, Annie and Clara that there is a woman stranger at the door who she doesn't like the look of particularly, 'She doesn't look up to much to me'.

Far more effective is to write:

Ruby tells Maria, Annie and Clara that there is a woman at the door, 'She doesn't look up to much to me'.

Always lay out the lines as they appear in the text. For example:

Clara is furious when Herbert says: 'It was only a bit of fun.'
CLARA: 'Oh – an' how long have you been 'aving these bits o' fun – as you call them – Herbert Soppitt?'

However, the most sophisticated way of using the writer's words is to embed them into your sentence:

Helliwell is horrified when Gerald says that the men and their wives 'have only been living together all this time'.

When you use quotations in this way, you are demonstrating the ability to use text as evidence to support your ideas - not simply including words from the original to prove you have read it.

Everyone writes differently. Work through the suggestions given here and adapt the advice to suit your own style and interests. This will improve your essay-writing skills and allow your personal voice to emerge.

The following points indicate in ascending order the skills of essay writing:

- Picking out one or two facts about the story and adding the odd detail
- Writing about the text by retelling the story
- Retelling the story and adding a quotation here and there
- Organising an answer which explains what is happening in the text and giving quotations to support what you write

....

- Writing in such a way as to show that you have thought about the intentions of the writer of the text and that you understand the techniques used
- Writing at some length, giving your viewpoint on the text and commenting by picking out details to support your views
- Looking at the text as a work of art, demonstrating clear critical judgement and explaining to the reader of your essay how the enjoyment of the text is assisted by literary devices, linguistic effects and psychological insights; showing how the text relates to the time when it was written

The dotted line above represents the division between lower and higher level grades. Higher-level performance begins when you start to consider your response as a reader of the text. The highest level is reached when you offer an enthusiastic personal response and show how this piece of literature is a product of its time.

Coursework essay

Set aside an hour or so at the start of your work to plan what you have to do.

- List all the points you feel are needed to cover the task. Collect page references of information and quotations that will support what you have to say. A helpful tool is the highlighter pen: this saves painstaking copying and enables you to target precisely what you want to use.
- Focus on what you consider to be the main points of the essay. Try to sum up your argument in a single sentence, which could be the closing sentence of your essay. Depending on the essay title, it could be a statement about a character: Clara Soppitt is one of the more forceful characters in *When We Are Married*. Examine her character in relationship to the other wives, her husband and Mrs Northrop; an opinion about setting: The description of the set at the beginning of Act I, and the prejudices of many of the main characters, help us to understand the pretentiousness underlying the comedy; or a judgement on a theme: I think one of the main themes of *When We Are Married* concerns itself with hypocrisy and self-delusion.
- Make a short essay plan. Use the first paragraph to introduce the argument you wish to make. In the following paragraphs develop this argument with details, examples and other possible points of view. Sum up your argument in the last paragraph. Check you have answered the question.
- Write the essay, remembering all the time the central point you are making.
- On completion, go back over what you have written to eliminate careless errors and improve expression. Read it aloud to yourself, or, if you are feeling more confident, to a relative or friend.

If you can, try to type your essay, using a word processor. This will allow you to correct and improve your writing without spoiling its appearance.

Examination essay

The essay written in an examination often carries more marks than the coursework essay even though it is written under considerable time pressure.

In the revision period build up notes on various aspects of the text you are using. Fortunately, in acquiring this York Notes on *When We Are Married*, you have made a prudent beginning! York Notes are set out to give you vital information and help you to construct your personal overview of the text.

Make notes with appropriate quotations about the key issues of the set text. Go into the examination knowing your text and having a clear set of opinions about it.

In most English Literature examinations you can take in copies of your set books. This in an enormous advantage although it may lull you into a false sense of security. Beware! There is simply not enough time in an examination to read the book from scratch.

In the examination

- Read the question paper carefully and remind yourself what you have to do.
- Look at the questions on your set texts to select the one that most interests you and mentally work out the points you wish to stress.
- Remind yourself of the time available and how you are going to use it.
- Briefly map out a short plan in note form that will keep your writing on track and illustrate the key argument you want to make.
- Then set about writing it.
- When you have finished, check through to eliminate errors.

To summarise, • Know the text
these are the • Have a clear understanding of and opinions on the storyline,
keys to success: characters, setting, themes and writer's concerns
            • Select the right material
            • Plan and write a clear response, continually bearing the question
              in mind

SAMPLE ESSAY PLAN

A typical essay question on *When We Are Married* is followed by a sample essay plan in note form. This does not present the only answer to the question, merely one answer. Do not be afraid to include your own ideas, and leave out some of those in the sample! Remember that quotations are essential to prove and illustrate the points you make.

Examine how several of the apparent minor characters crucially influence the course of the comedy.

Such a question demands that you should start by stating your chosen characters and tracing the course of each one on the development of the play. Note that the wording of such a question does not permit for disagreement on the part of the candidate!

Part 1:
Introduction

Write down the characters you have selected, in this case, Gerald Forbes, Henry Ormonroyd and Lottie Grady and a brief comment on their role in the play. Then take each character in turn.

Part 2:
Gerald Forbes

• A description of Gerald Forbes and mention of his relationship with Nancy Holmes, Joseph Helliwell's niece.
• His influence in the first part of the play.
• His confrontation with Helliwell, Parker and Soppitt.
• His revelation about their marriage.
• How this quickly changes the attitudes, especially of Helliwell and Parker, to him.

- More or less disappears from the scene as an influential character after this.

Part 3: Henry
Ormonroyd

- A description of Henry Ormonroyd, his fondness for drink, his fuddled amiability.
- His influence in the first part of the play: his first appearance in dialogue with Ruby and Nancy allows the playwright to further our knowledge of situation and character.
- The interlude in Act II where he slurringly talks to Ruby again. Gives him an opportunity to comment on his own marriage and marriage in general.

Part 4: Lottie
Grady

- A description of Lottie Grady.
- How she is thought of by Ruby and the other women?
- Her unexpected appearance on the scene and her motives.
- Her purposely baiting Maria, Annie and Clara.
- How serious is she in her designs on Joseph Helliwell? If it is light-hearted then we can understand her horror when Maria Helliwell threatens to leave.

Part 5:
Conclusion

- It is the minor character of Gerald Forbes who creates the 'drama' of the play in Act I.
- However, the latter part and the resolution of the ending of the play is greatly influenced by Lottie and Ormonroyd.
- Lottie and Ormonroyd have obviously known one another for some time, but we assume they have lost touch.
- Lottie is instrumental in revealing that Ormonroyd has something to tell them of interest.
- Ormonroyd solves the dilemma and all ends happily.
- Ironically, it is Ormonroyd, the most disreputable character in the play, along with Lottie, seen as 'a loose woman', who solve the problem for those with

SAMPLE ESSAY PLAN continued

social pretensions who consider themselves a cut above others.

This is by no means an exhaustive or definitive answer to the question. However, looked at in conjunction with the general notes on Essay Writing, it does show you the way your mind should be working in order to produce a reasonably thorough essay.

FURTHER QUESTIONS

Make a plan as shown above and attempt these questions.

1 Examine the different ways in which the three couples react to Gerald's news.
2 Suggest ways in which Priestley makes us laugh in this play.
3 Examine the characters of Joseph Helliwell, Albert Parker and Herbert Soppitt. How far do their characters and attitudes differ?
4 Suggest some of the aspects of society that the playwright criticises in this comedy.
5 Describe the way in which Priestley presents the character of Ruby Birtle throughout the play.
6 Which of the characters do you find most likeable in the play and why?
7 Describe the differences between the characters and attitudes of Maria Helliwell, Annie Parker and Clara Soppitt.
8 What aspects of the play fix it in the early twentieth century?
9 What do the characters of Henry Ormonroyd and Lottie Grady add to the play and its action?
10 Examine the purpose of such apparently 'minor' characters as Gerald Forbes, Nancy Holmes and Fred Dyson.

Cultural Connections

Broader Perspectives

When We Are Married is a comedy of a particular type. It is not a **high comedy** of manners nor a **drawing-room comedy** but a comedy of more or less ordinary people involved in ordinary everyday concerns – sometimes referred to as **low comedy** (see Literary Terms). The language is **colloquial** (see Literary Terms) with a successful attempt to imitate regional accent and vocabulary. The central dilemma of the invalid marriage is of course the stuff of farce as is the wandering in and out of the increasingly drunken Henry Ormonroyd. Yet it is not so exaggerated as to become absurd or **melodramatic** (see Literary Terms), nor is it slap-stick.

With nearly all of us familiar with television, we can see elements, events and characters similar to such a series as *Last of the Summer Wine*. This tradition goes back much further in the history of the theatre, of course. A play such as the nineteenth-century Russian writer Gogol's play *The Government Inspector* contains self-delusion and pretentiousness – even if on a more extended scale than in Priestley's play.

Puritan severity was once confused with virtue and duty. We see this especially in the attitudes of Helliwell and Parker as elders of the Chapel. Yet their stance is misguided because even as they are criticising Gerald Forbes for unacceptable behaviour in the eyes of the community and the Chapel, they have been over-indulging themselves at a feast. Their self-righteousness is somewhat of a sham in the face of their pomposity.

The invalid marriage after twenty-five years is a device for mirth and for them to be forced to make a re-examination of their lives and relationships. Even so, the characters remain realistic enough to be credible. Perhaps we recognise people we know in some of the characters. If we are honest, we may even see some reflection of ourselves and our attitudes here and there. I am sure we all know of a Joseph Helliwell or Clara Soppitt, for example!

The great and continuing success of the play is largely because it is well crafted. In its first performances in 1938 and 1939 it made a welcome diversion for the theatregoer from the Munich crisis and the threat of the coming Second World War. It still remains popular today with both amateur and professional companies.

If you are interested to find out more about J.B. Priestley and his works you might like to consult some of the books in the following list:

David Hughes, *J.B. Priestley: An Informal Study of his Work*, Hart Davis, 1958

The Plays of J.B. Priestley, 3 vols, Heinemann, 1962

Gareth Lloyd Evans, *J.B. Priestley: The Dramatist*, Heinemann, 1964

Susan Cook, *J.B. Priestley: Portrait of an Author*, Heinemann, 1970

J.B. Priestley, *Instead of the Trees: A Final Chapter in Autobiography*, Heinemann, 1977

John Braine, *J.B. Priestley*, Weidenfeld and Nicholson, 1978

Vincent Brome, *J.B. Priestley*, Hamish Hamilton, 1988
Judith Cook, *Priestley*, Bloomsbury, 1997

Chekov (1860–1904) Russian author and playwright. His works present a picture of mankind at the mercy of forces outside and beyond their control. The 'little man' against the universe

colloquialism the use of kinds of expression and grammar associated with ordinary, everyday speech rather then formal language

comedy, high comedy of wit, intellect and manners

comedy, low causing humour by the simplest of means e.g. verbal (puns), situation and character

comic causing laughter – either sympathetic or scornful

dénouement the final unravelling of the complications of the plot

dialogue speech and conversation between characters

didactic teaching or instructing

domestic drama a play whose setting is in a family or household

dramatic irony when the audience (or some of the characters in the play as well) has more information about what is happening than a character

drawing-room drama a play set in the drawing-room of usually a middle to upper middle class house; usually a comedy of manners. Very much in vogue in the 1920s and 1930s

farce/farcical comedy one that uses exaggerated characters and complicated plots with, perhaps, ludicrous situations

implication that which is hinted at or implied

irony saying something when you mean the opposite e.g. Gerald 'Is that all?' (p. 3) when he actually means: 'Surely that's enough?'

melodrama sensational drama with violent appeal to the emotions and a happy ending

Messiah oratorio by Handel (1685–1769); very popular around Christmas time especially in Northern

England where it is almost an institution

naturalistic tradition literature in which mankind is seen as subject to natural forces such as heredity or environment; social, spiritual and intellectual aspirations are regarded as meaningless; typical subject matter is the miserable, poverty-stricken life of the characters or meaningless tragedy. Against this Priestley's writing is light relief!

nostalgia a mood of sadness associated with a wish to return to the past

nouveau riche a derisive term for those, especially of a lower class, who have made money and have the pretensions to be of a better standing than they are

personify/personification treating abstract things or ideas as if they had animal or human characteristics

provincial uncultured, clumsy, not up-to-date

radical wishing to change society 'at root'; having views that are considered to verge on the extreme

realist school literature that attempts to show things as they really are; a practical outlook on life

repartee a witty, swift reply, often mildly insulting; frequent in comic drama e.g. Ruby and Ormonroyd (pp. 47–51)

socialist a belief in an economic theory that production is for use rather than profit, that there should be equality of individual wealth and an absence of competitive economic activity

stage directions instructions in the text or information about the setting of the play and indications to the performers about character, movement and attitudes

transience that which is momentary or passing

West Riding the county of Yorkshire in Northern England was originally divided into 'thriddings' which meant 'three parts'. These were the North, East and West Riding

TEST ANSWERS

TEST YOURSELF (Act I)

A 1 Ruby Birtle
... 2 Mrs Northrop
3 Alderman Joseph Helliwell
4 Councillor Albert Parker
5 Maria Helliwell
6 Gerald Forbes
7 Herbert Soppitt

TEST YOURSELF (Act II)

A 1 Clara Soppitt
... 2 Mrs Northrop
3 Fred Dyson

4 Henry Ormonroyd
5 Mrs Northrop
6 Alderman Joseph Helliwell
7 Lottie Grady

TEST YOURSELF (Act III)

A 1 Nancy Holmes
... 2 Councillor Albert Parker
3 Annie Parker
4 Herbert Soppitt
5 Lottie Grady's 'our Violet'
6 Mrs Northrop

GCSE and equivalent levels (£3.50 each)

Maya Angelou
I Know Why the Caged Bird Sings

Jane Austen
Pride and Prejudice

Alan Ayckbourn
Absent Friends

Elizabeth Barrett Browning
Selected Poems

Robert Bolt
A Man for All Seasons

Harold Brighouse
Hobson's Choice

Charlotte Brontë
Jane Eyre

Emily Brontë
Wuthering Heights

Shelagh Delaney
A Taste of Honey

Charles Dickens
David Copperfield

Charles Dickens
Great Expectations

Charles Dickens
Hard Times

Charles Dickens
Oliver Twist

Roddy Doyle
Paddy Clarke Ha Ha Ha

George Eliot
Silas Marner

George Eliot
The Mill on the Floss

Anne Frank
The Diary of Anne Frank

William Golding
Lord of the Flies

Oliver Goldsmith
She Stoops To Conquer

Willis Hall
The Long and the Short and the Tall

Thomas Hardy
Far from the Madding Crowd

Thomas Hardy
The Mayor of Casterbridge

Thomas Hardy
Tess of the d'Urbervilles

Thomas Hardy
The Withered Arm and other Wessex Tales

L.P. Hartley
The Go-Between

Seamus Heaney
Selected Poems

Susan Hill
I'm the King of the Castle

Barry Hines
A Kestrel for a Knave

Louise Lawrence
Children of the Dust

Harper Lee
To Kill a Mockingbird

Laurie Lee
Cider with Rosie

Arthur Miller
The Crucible

Arthur Miller
A View from the Bridge

Robert O'Brien
Z for Zachariah

Frank O'Connor
My Oedipus Complex and Other Stories

George Orwell
Animal Farm

J.B. Priestley
An Inspector Calls

J.B. Priestley
When We Are Married

Willy Russell
Educating Rita

Willy Russell
Our Day Out

J.D. Salinger
The Catcher in the Rye

William Shakespeare
Henry IV Part 1

William Shakespeare
Henry V

William Shakespeare
Julius Caesar

William Shakespeare
Macbeth

William Shakespeare
The Merchant of Venice

William Shakespeare
A Midsummer Night's Dream

William Shakespeare
Much Ado About Nothing

William Shakespeare
Romeo and Juliet

William Shakespeare
The Tempest

William Shakespeare
Twelfth Night

George Bernard Shaw
Pygmalion

Mary Shelley
Frankenstein

R.C. Sherriff
Journey's End

Rukshana Smith
Salt on the Snow

John Steinbeck
Of Mice and Men

Robert Louis Stevenson
Dr Jekyll and Mr Hyde

Jonathan Swift
Gulliver's Travels

Robert Swindells
Daz 4 Zoe

Mildred D. Taylor
Roll of Thunder, Hear My Cry

Mark Twain
Huckleberry Finn

James Watson
Talking in Whispers

Edith Wharton
Ethan Frome

William Wordsworth
Selected Poems

A Choice of Poets

Mystery Stories of the Nineteenth Century including The Signalman

Nineteenth Century Short Stories

Poetry of the First World War

Six Women Poets

GCSE and equivalent levels (£3.50 each)

Maya Angelou
I Know Why the Caged Bird Sings

Jane Austen
Pride and Prejudice

Alan Ayckbourn
Absent Friends

Elizabeth Barrett Browning
Selected Poems

Robert Bolt
A Man for All Seasons

Harold Brighouse
Hobson's Choice

Charlotte Brontë
Jane Eyre

Emily Brontë
Wuthering Heights

Shelagh Delaney
A Taste of Honey

Charles Dickens
David Copperfield

Charles Dickens
Great Expectations

Charles Dickens
Hard Times

Charles Dickens
Oliver Twist

Roddy Doyle
Paddy Clarke Ha Ha Ha

George Eliot
Silas Marner

George Eliot
The Mill on the Floss

Anne Frank
The Diary of Anne Frank

William Golding
Lord of the Flies

Oliver Goldsmith
She Stoops To Conquer

Willis Hall
The Long and the Short and the Tall

Thomas Hardy
Far from the Madding Crowd

Thomas Hardy
The Mayor of Casterbridge

Thomas Hardy
Tess of the d'Urbervilles

Thomas Hardy
The Withered Arm and other Wessex Tales

L.P. Hartley
The Go-Between

Seamus Heaney
Selected Poems

Susan Hill
I'm the King of the Castle

Barry Hines
A Kestrel for a Knave

Louise Lawrence
Children of the Dust

Harper Lee
To Kill a Mockingbird

Laurie Lee
Cider with Rosie

Arthur Miller
The Crucible

Arthur Miller
A View from the Bridge

Robert O'Brien
Z for Zachariah

Frank O'Connor
My Oedipus Complex and Other Stories

George Orwell
Animal Farm

J.B. Priestley
An Inspector Calls

J.B. Priestley
When We Are Married

Willy Russell
Educating Rita

Willy Russell
Our Day Out

J.D. Salinger
The Catcher in the Rye

William Shakespeare
Henry IV Part 1

William Shakespeare
Henry V

William Shakespeare
Julius Caesar

William Shakespeare
Macbeth

William Shakespeare
The Merchant of Venice

William Shakespeare
A Midsummer Night's Dream

William Shakespeare
Much Ado About Nothing

William Shakespeare
Romeo and Juliet

William Shakespeare
The Tempest

William Shakespeare
Twelfth Night

George Bernard Shaw
Pygmalion

Mary Shelley
Frankenstein

R.C. Sherriff
Journey's End

Rukshana Smith
Salt on the Snow

John Steinbeck
Of Mice and Men

Robert Louis Stevenson
Dr Jekyll and Mr Hyde

Jonathan Swift
Gulliver's Travels

Robert Swindells
Daz 4 Zoe

Mildred D. Taylor
Roll of Thunder, Hear My Cry

Mark Twain
Huckleberry Finn

James Watson
Talking in Whispers

Edith Wharton
Ethan Frome

William Wordsworth
Selected Poems

A Choice of Poets

Mystery Stories of the Nineteenth Century including The Signalman

Nineteenth Century Short Stories

Poetry of the First World War

Six Women Poets

FUTURE TITLES IN THE YORK NOTES SERIES

Jane Austen
Emma

Jane Austen
Sense and Sensibility

Samuel Beckett
Waiting for Godot and
Endgame

Louis de Bernières
Captain Corelli's Mandolin

Charlotte Brontë
Villette

Caryl Churchill
Top Girls and *Cloud Nine*

Charles Dickens
Bleak House

T.S. Eliot
The Waste Land

Thomas Hardy
Jude the Obscure

Homer
The Iliad

Homer
The Odyssey

Aldous Huxley
Brave New World

D.H. Lawrence
Selected Poems

Christopher Marlowe
Edward II

George Orwell
Nineteen Eighty-four

Jean Rhys
Wide Sargasso Sea

William Shakespeare
Henry IV Pt I

William Shakespeare
Henry IV Part II

William Shakespeare
Macbeth

William Shakespeare
Richard III

Tom Stoppard
Arcadia and *Rosencrantz and
Guildenstern are Dead*

Virgil
The Aeneid

Jeanette Winterson
*Oranges are Not the Only
Fruit*

Tennessee Williams
Cat on a Hot Tin Roof

Metaphysical Poets

NOTES